The Big Green Book of the Big Blue Sea

Written by
Helaine Becker

Illustrated by
Willow Dawson

Kids Can Press

The author acknowledges the support of the Ontario Arts Council in the creation of this project.

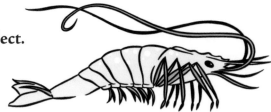

Kids Can Press acknowledges the financial support of the Government of Ontario, through the Ontario Media Development Corporation's Ontario Book Initiative; the Ontario Arts Council; the Canada Council for the Arts; and the Government of Canada, through the BPIDP, for our publishing activity.

Published in Canada by
Kids Can Press Ltd.
25 Dockside Drive
Toronto, ON M5A 0B5

Published in the U.S. by
Kids Can Press Ltd.
2250 Military Road
Tonawanda, NY 14150

www.kidscanpress.com

Edited by Karen Li
Designed by Julia Naimska

The hardcover edition of this book is smyth sewn casebound.
The paperback edition of this book is limp sewn with a drawn-on cover.
Manufactured in Buji, Shenzhen, China, in 11/2011 by WKT Company

CM 12 0 9 8 7 6 5 4 3 2 1
CM PA 12 0 9 8 7 6 5 4 3 2 1

Photo credits
Every reasonable effort has been made to trace ownership of, and give accurate credit to, copyrighted material. Information that would enable the publisher to correct any discrepancies in future editions would be appreciated.

p. 9: Irina Opachevsky/Photos.com; **p. 13:** Michel Lizarzaburu/Photos.com; **p. 21:** Richard Carey/Photos.com; **p. 25:** © iStockphoto.com/ Justin Reznick; **p. 28:** Artem Zhushman/Photos.com; **p. 31:** Luna Vandoorne/Shutterstock.com; **p. 33:** U.S. Coast Guard photo by Ensign Jason Radcliffe; **p. 35:** U.S. Coast Guard photo; **p. 39:** © iStockphoto.com/Heike Loos; **p. 45:** Zeamonkey/Photos.com; **p. 46:** Richard Carey/ Photos.com; **p. 49:** Porsteinn Asgeirsson/Photos.com; **p. 56:** Jupiterimages/Photos.com; **p. 57:** Ablestock.com/ Photos.com; **p. 59:** Raldi Somers/Photos.com; **p. 61:** Mikhail Kokhanchikov/Photos.com; **p. 65:** Cornelis Opstal/Photos.com; **p. 66:** Amanda Cotton/Photos.com; **p. 73:** John Anderson/Photos.com; **p. 75:** Pui Yee Ling/ Photos.com; **p. 77:** (top) Andrey Armyagov/Photos.com, (bottom) Photos.com/Getty Images

Library and Archives Canada Cataloguing in Publication

Becker, Helaine, 1961–

    The big green book of the big blue sea / written by Helaine Becker ; illustrated by Willow Dawson.

Includes index.

ISBN 978-1-55453-746-4 (bound)
ISBN 978-1-55453-747-1 (pbk.)

1. Ocean — Juvenile literature. 2. Marine ecology — Juvenile literature.

3. Marine pollution — Juvenile literature. I. Dawson, Willow II. Title.

GC1090.B43 2012   j577.7'27   C2011-905526-0

Kids Can Press is a **Corus**™ Entertainment company

Contents

What Is the Ocean?

Whether you live on the beach or a thousand kilometers inland, the ocean is the most important thing in your life.

Don't believe it? Your ancestors — the ancestors of all living things — evolved in the sea. The oxygen you breathe was produced by plankton that live in the sea. Most of the carbon dioxide you exhale is absorbed by the sea.

You cannot live without the ocean. Your blood, sweat and tears are all versions of seawater we carry within us so we can survive on land. Ultimately, every bit of you, even the minerals in your bones, will one day return to the sea.

So what *is* this ocean? What is it made of? And how does it work?

Most simply, the ocean is a vast body of salt water. It's also the support system for the worldwide web of life. And it's our planet's engine, helping to circulate the magma in its core and the atmosphere at its fringes.

If Earth were a living creature, the rock beneath your feet would be its skeleton, the atmosphere would be its lungs, and the ocean would be its life's blood.

For millions and millions of years, the ocean didn't change much. Its temperature, acidity and oxygen levels all remained incredibly stable. That stability allowed life to develop and flourish.

But the ocean today is changing. Human activity has caused transformations not seen since the age of dinosaurs. The ocean is getting warmer. It's becoming more acidic. Vast areas of the ocean are even being depleted of oxygen.

These transformations have already begun to affect life in the ocean. They will soon begin to affect life on land, too. The ocean is so important to all of Earth's creatures and processes that one plain fact becomes clear: If the ocean isn't healthy, then nothing else on Earth can be healthy.

But the news is not all bad. People all over the world are beginning to take action to help protect our oceans. In this book, you'll find out what they're doing — and the ways in which *you* can make a difference, no matter how far you live from the sea.

You'll also discover how the ocean functions in the best possible way — by rolling up your sleeves and *doing*. Try the fun, easy activities on these pages. Meet a few of the fascinating animals that call the ocean home. Experiment with some of the incredible adaptations they use to survive. (Expect lots of splashing!)

With this book as your guide, you'll better understand the ocean and its threats. We hope it will also inspire you to develop ideas of your own that will contribute to the long-term health of the ocean.

Our Big Blue ... Basketball?

Most of Earth is covered with oceans. Score a better idea of how wet Earth really is when you try this activity.

You Will Need

- a roll of blue 2.5 cm (1 in.) wide tape
- ruler
- scissors
- a basketball

1 Measure off 726 cm (286 in.) of tape. Cut the tape into short strips as you measure it. Stick the strips along the edge of a table until you have them all ready.

2 Here's the tricky part: Stick all of the pieces of tape to the basketball — but don't let any of the tape overlap!

3 There! You did it! Does your basketball now look mostly orange — or mostly blue?

What's Going On?

About 75 percent of the Earth's surface is covered with water, just like 75 percent of your basketball is covered with tape.

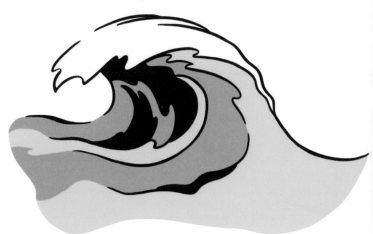

What's Happening Now?

We know there's plenty of saltwater out there. But what about freshwater? Not so much. Less than 3 percent of the earth's water is actually drinkable!

About one-sixth of the world's people lack access to fresh, clean water for cooking and drinking. Five million die every year because of it. As the world's population grows and demand for freshwater increases, the shortage is getting worse.

What Can You Do?

One way to deal with the drinking water shortage is simply to waste less of the wet stuff. In the 1990s, New York City was faced with having to build a new water pumping station to meet growing water needs. Instead, the city got residents to replace older, water-hogging toilets with low-flow ones. Over one million new toilets later, the city saved 265–340 million L (70–90 million U.S. gal.) of water a day!

You can save water, too, with or without installing a new toilet. Try these simple, effective, start-right-now steps:

- Turn off the water when scrubbing your pearly whites and save 15 L (4 U.S. gal.) a minute.
- Tossing a tissue? Use the wastebasket instead of flushing it and save 20 L (5 U.S. gal.) for each flush.

- Take a shower instead of a bath and save 160 L (40 U.S. gal.).
- Is there a water-saving showerhead on your shower? If so, it will save 10 L (3 U.S. gal.) a minute each time you take a shower!
- In the shower, turn off the water when you lather up your shampoo — save 40 L (10 U.S. gal.).
- Cleaning your 40 L (10 U.S. gal.) fish tank? Use the old water to feed your houseplants and save 40 L (10 U.S. gal.)! And when you refill Fido's water dish, give the old water to those thirsty plants, too!

The Big Rock Candy Mountain

What makes the ocean salty? Find out with this sweet experiment.

You Will Need

- sugar cubes (about 24)
- icing
- a small plate
- plastic building blocks
- a baking dish
- a cup

1 Each sugar cube is a "rock." Stick the cubes together with icing. Pile them on your plate until you have created a mini mountain.

2 Place your plastic building blocks into the baking dish in a single layer. Set the plate with the mountain on top of the bricks.

3 Fill a cup with warm water. Slowly pour it over your mountain. Repeat until the baking dish has about 1.5 cm (5/8 in.) of water in it.

4 Look at your mountain. Is it the same size and shape as it was before the "rainstorms"? Dip your finger into the water in the baking dish. How does it taste?

5 Repeat the "rainstorms" for the next few days. How do you think the water will taste each time?

What's Going On?

Rocks are made up of many minerals. The most common one is sodium chloride. That's the stuff table salt is made of.

Rocks are constantly exposed to the effects of weather — rain, ice, snow and wind. They begin to erode, or break down. The salt they contain gets dissolved, just like the sugar in the cubes. Running water carries it away in rivers or streams. The salt eventually makes its way to the ocean.

Land isn't the only source of ocean salt. Another source is the ocean itself! Rock from deep in the Earth's mantle comes to the surface of the ocean floor at underwater vents (see page 24). The salt in them then dissolves to add its savor to the oceanic soup.

What's Happening Now?

One solution to water shortage might come from an unlikely source — the sea! Desalination plants — factories that remove the salt from seawater — have operated around the world since the 1960s. They use two main methods. The first method uses heat to separate the salt from the water. In the second method, saltwater is forced through a membrane — a sandwich of both thin and thick plastic-like materials with microscopic pores. The pores allow water to pass through, but they trap the larger salt molecules.

Both methods of desalination use a lot of electricity. That makes them expensive to run. And since they burn fossil fuels to create electricity, the plants also contribute to global warming.

A team of researchers has recently come up with a "bright" alternative to energy-hogging plants. Instead of building huge factories to desalinate water, why not deploy small, portable desalinators that run on the sun? The inventors say that their solar-powered mini-system can produce up to 300 L (80 U.S. gal.) of drinkable water a day. It is also being designed so that even non-scientists can put one together and get it running in a flash.

The Dead Sea is one of the saltiest bodies of water on earth. When its waters evaporate in the hot sun, mounds of crystallized salt are left behind.

Ocean Layer Cake

Water gets into the ocean in many ways — from streams and rivers, rain and snow. It can be hot or cold. It can contain lots of minerals or very few. But what happens once it reaches the sea? Does it all mix together like a giant bowl of soup? To find out, try this colorful experiment.

You Will Need

- 2 cups
- a 2-cup measuring cup
- 3 ice cubes
- 125 mL (1/2 c.) table salt
- food coloring (green, blue and red)
- a turkey baster

1 Mix 125 mL (1/2 c.) of water with the ice in one cup. Add 50 mL (1/4 c.) salt to the ice water. Stir until most of the salt is dissolved. Add a few drops of green food coloring.

2 In a second cup, mix 125 mL (1/2 c.) lukewarm water with 50 mL (1/4 c.) of salt. Stir until most of the salt is dissolved. Color this mixture blue.

3 Measure 75 ml (1/3 c.) very hot tap water in the measuring cup. Color this water red.

4 Suck up some cold, green water with the baster. Place its tip at the bottom of the cup of red water. Slowly squeeze the bulb to let all the green water out. Keep squeezing the bulb until you've removed the baster from the measuring cup.

5 Suck up some blue water with the baster. Place the tip of the baster into the cup, at the borderline of the red and green water. Slowly release the blue water.

6 Do the colors mix? Or do you have a three-color Ocean Layer Cake?

10

What's Going On?

In the ocean, different water densities don't mix. They form distinct layers, just like in your measuring cup. Denser water sinks. Less dense water floats on the denser water below it.

How dense water is depends on its temperature and what's mixed into it:

- Salt water is denser than freshwater.
- Cold water is denser than hot water.

At the top of the ocean is a warm layer called the Sunlit Zone. The next layer down, the Twilight Zone, is cooler, saltier and denser. Below that is the even colder, even saltier and even denser Midnight Zone. And down at the very bottom are the darkest, coldest, saltiest layers of all, the Abyssal Zone and the Deep Trenches.

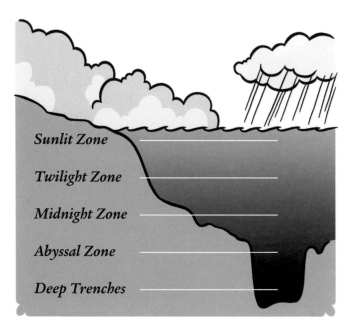

Sunlit Zone

Twilight Zone

Midnight Zone

Abyssal Zone

Deep Trenches

What's Happening Now?

A new technology called Ocean Thermal Energy Conversion (OTEC) takes advantage of the ocean's layers to generate energy.

First, warm surface water is used to heat a liquid with a low boiling point, like ammonia. The gas the ammonia gives off drives a turbine to generate electricity. The gas is then cooled so it can be reused. The cooling agent? Cold seawater pumped from the deepest ocean layers!

OTEC is a promising new source of clean, renewable energy. But it isn't perfect. Researchers are still trying to make OTEC safer, more efficient and less expensive so it can be used more widely.

Brrrine Adventure

Does brine (salty water) freeze faster than freshwater? Find out when you try this freezie race game — no overcoat required!

You Will Need

- 2 containers (such as empty yogurt tubs)
- 2 unfrozen freezies (plastic-wrapped Popsicles)
- crushed ice
- 500 mL (2 c.) rock salt

1 Put one freezie in each container. Pour crushed ice around both freezies.

2 Add the salt to just one of the containers. Stir the ice and salt together so it's well mixed.

3 Which freezie will freeze faster, the one in the salt and ice mixture, or the one in the plain ice? To find out, check both freezies every five minutes. The winner is the freezie that's ready to eat first!

What's Going On?

Freshwater freezes at 0°C (32°F). Saltwater, however, doesn't freeze unless it's a few degrees colder (how much colder depends on how much salt there is in the water). Typical seawater freezes at −2.2°C (28°F).

When you put the room-temperature freezie into the plain ice, the ice drew heat from the freezie. At the same time, the freezie drew cold from the ice. The ice starts to melt when the temperature in the container hits 0°C (32°F). At that same temperature, the freezie starts to freeze.

Molecules with more energy (the hotter ones) transfer energy to molecules with less energy (colder ones) until they all have the same energy (that is, the same temperature).

Meanwhile, over in the salty container, the same kind of heat exchange is happening. But since the freezing point of salty water is lower than that of freshwater, the salty ice melts at a colder temperature than plain ice. Its melted water is also colder.

The colder, salty melted water draws more heat from the freezie than the fresh melted water. That makes the freezie in the salt and ice mixture freeze faster!

The Ocean at Risk

In June 2009, the world's oceans reached an average temperature of 17°C (62.6°F) — their highest since scientists began recording it in the nineteenth century. In a 2010 study of corals in the South Pacific, researchers discovered the first clear evidence linking rising ocean temperatures to human-caused global warming.

Warmer oceans can have serious consequences for both marine life and life on land. Rising temperatures alter the numbers of plankton — the microorganisms at the base of the marine food chain. Animals that cannot travel (such as coral) can overheat and die. Animals that move to cooler waters disrupt the rest of the food chain. And animals that migrate along fixed paths, like whales or sea turtles, may have trouble finding their traditional food sources.

Warmer oceans affect the climate on land, too. They may trigger more powerful and frequent tropical storms.

Iceberg!

Cold water is denser than warm water, so it sinks. But what about ice? Does it float or sink? To find out, build your own iceberg and test it against the "Titanic" next time you take a bath.

You Will Need

- a large plastic bag (ziplock bags work well)
- a twist tie or rubber band
- a toy boat

1 Fill the plastic bag with water. Tie the top using the rubber band or twist tie to make a rough pyramid shape. Leave it in the freezer until frozen solid. *Voila!* Instant iceberg.

2 Fill your bathtub with water. Plunk in the boat. Plunk yourself in, too.

3 Slip your iceberg into the tub. Does it float or sink?

4 Take a closer look at the 'berg. How much of the ice is poking above the water? How much is hiding below the surface?

5 How close can your boat get to the visible 'berg before it smacks into the ice below the surface?

What's Going On?

Water is really weird. Most other materials get denser when they freeze. But water does the opposite — it *expands* when it freezes.

This happens because water molecules have an interesting shape (interesting for molecules, that is). When they freeze in cold temperature, the shapes connect to form a regular, repeating 3-D pattern called a "tetrahedral lattice." Notice how much empty space there is between the frozen water molecules.

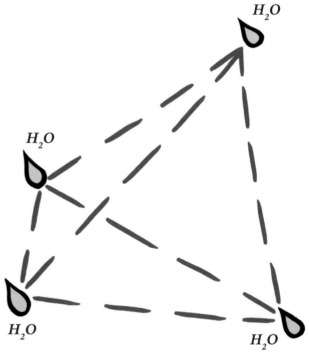

A single water molecule is made up of one atom of oxygen (O) and two atoms of hydrogen (H). Frozen together, they form a single ice crystal.

When ice melts, the individual water molecules are suddenly free to move around. They can even pack themselves more closely together than when they were frozen in the lattice. And that's exactly what liquid water molecules do. They pack together more closely than ice molecules.

Because liquid water has less space between its molecules than ice does, it's denser. That means ice will float on it!

This water weirdness makes life on Earth possible. Imagine the opposite situation, if frozen water were denser than liquid. During cold weather, ice would form on the surface of the ocean, but then sink to the bottom. A new layer of ice would form. It, too, would sink, and so on until all the oceans freeze.

A liquid ocean allowed life to evolve into the millions of forms we see today. So next time you slip on the ice, say thanks! It's that same slippery stuff that made *you* possible.

Try It!

Want to see for yourself how water expands when it freezes? Fill a plastic bottle about three-quarters full with water. Use a permanent marker to mark the water level. Put the bottle in the freezer (with the top off), and leave it until it is completely frozen. Then check your bottle. Has the waterline risen?

Global Warming, the Ocean and You

Sea ice is important for keeping Earth's climate steady. Because it is lighter in color than open water, it absorbs less heat from the sun. That helps keep the entire planet cooler.

Sea ice is also important to the survival of many kinds of animals. Polar bears, for example, walk on sea ice when they hunt for prey. If sea ice shrinks or breaks up earlier in spring, polar bears have fewer chances to hunt and a greater chance they will go hungry or die. Many people who live in the Arctic also depend on the sea ice for their livelihood.

Unfortunately, researchers have found evidence that sea ice in the Arctic is shrinking — about 8 percent a decade since 1953. Plus, the ice has been getting thinner. That means it will now melt even faster than before. The more sea ice melts, the more quickly global warming could speed up. The warmer Earth gets, the more ice melts ... and the warmer things become ... you get the picture.

In Arctic Canada, the changes to sea ice have been very dramatic. The most dramatic change of all, perhaps, involves the Northwest Passage, a high Arctic sea route that is usually covered with ice. In 2007, it briefly became fully navigable — free of ice — *for the first time in recorded history*.

Shipping companies may love the idea of a quicker route between Europe and Asia. But local people and environmentalists are concerned about the opening of the channel. They worry about the effects more traffic and more tourism may have on their fragile ecosystem. They also worry about how warming temperatures may affect the Arctic in the long term.

What Can You Do?

Help keep the ocean cool by using less of the kinds of energy that contribute to global warming. That means using fewer appliances or gadgets that run on electricity or fossil fuels. Here are some examples:

- Instead of getting a car ride to a friend's house, take a bike, use public transit, rollerskate or walk.
- Organize a "walking school bus" with your friends. The kid who lives farthest from school goes to the next kid's house and so on, picking up "passengers" along the way. You'll be safe, have fun AND save energy.
- Feeling chilly? Don't automatically turn up the heat. Grab a sweater instead.
- Addicted to video games? Set yourself a time limit. When your time is up, switch to a different kind of game that doesn't use electricity.
- Make sure you turn the lights off whenever you leave a room (and the TV and your computer, too!). This simple change alone can prevent tons of energy from being wasted.

The Engine of the Ocean

Sure (or should we say "shore"), water separates into different layers in the ocean. But that doesn't mean it always stays put. In fact, ocean water moves around a lot. So much so, in fact, that it acts like an engine, driving activity in and out of the sea in many ways.

Explore "current events" when you make this ocean-motion model.

You Will Need

- a glass loaf pan
- 2 cups
- ice
- food coloring (blue and red)
- 2 eye droppers

1 Fill the loaf pan with room-temperature water.

2 In one cup, mix water with ice until it is very cold. Add a few drops of blue food coloring to the ice water.

3 In the second cup, mix very hot water with some red food coloring.

4 Fill one dropper with red water and one with blue.

5 Squeeze the hot red water into the left side of the loaf pan and the cold blue water into the right at the same time. What happens in the pan?

What's Going On?

When you squeeze the colored water into the tank, the warm water rises to the top and the cold water sinks to the bottom. (Cold water is denser than warm water, right?)

The cold water spreads out on the bottom of the loaf pan, pushing the water that was already there ahead of it. When that water reaches the other side, it is forced to mingle with some of the warmer (red-tinted) water. The cold water gets a bit warmer. It starts to rise.

Meanwhile, on the other side of the loaf pan, the warm water meets the cold water. It starts to cool. As it cools, it sinks, pushing the blue water along its path even faster than before. A cycle forms in which the blue water pushes the red water, which pushes the blue water, and so on.

The circular, moving pathway is called a convection current. Convection currents are common wherever you have a source of heat and a fluid (air, water, even melted rock!).

What's Happening Now?

The ocean has oodles of convection currents. Fueled by cold water from the poles and warm water near the equator, they keep the entire ocean in constant motion.

The separate currents all join together in what's been nicknamed the Global Conveyer Belt. Over the course of several thousand years, the conveyor belt circulates every water molecule in the ocean to all corners of the globe.

Convection currents have a large effect on marine life. When cold water rises from the ocean floor, it brings with it nutrients that have sunk to the bottom. Regions where these upwellings occur are prime feeding grounds for many sea animals. Whales, for example, feed on phytoplankton and krill brought up from the depths by upwellings off the coast of Newfoundland.

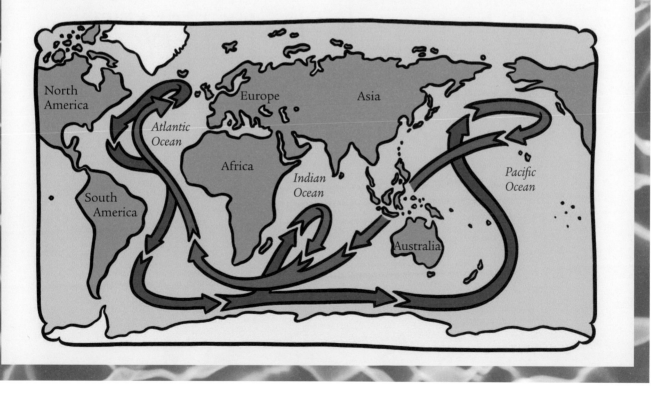

The Great Pacific Garbage Patch

Find out what happens to all the bits and pieces of plastic people throw away once they get to the sea.

You Will Need

• worn out plastic bags, both clear and white
• scissors

1 Cut the bags into random-sized strips.

2 With the bathtub tap on, dribble bits of plastic into the running water. Watch how the plastic moves. Does it float?

3 When you've added all the plastic, turn off the tap. (You only need a few centimeters, or inches, of water to see the plastic float.) Push the water along one side of the tub to get the water moving in a circle around the tub. This mimics the way currents move in different parts of the sea.

4 Does your plastic tend to collect in one part of the tub?

What's Going On?

Every year, bits of plastic — TONS of it — get blown or washed into the sea. Plastic takes a long time to break down, so most of it bobs on the surface for many years.

Circular currents, like the one you created in the bathtub, force floating objects to collect in the middle. That's why your shredded plastic may have formed a single blob in the center of your tub.

In many parts of the ocean, circular currents called gyres work the same way. They form long-lasting "islands" of plastic in the middle of the sea.

The biggest plastic island is called the Great Pacific Garbage Patch. No one knows how big it is exactly, but most estimates suggest it is roughly twice the size of the state of Texas, and growing.

The Great Pacific Garbage Patch is more than just ugly. It's also dangerous. Plastics leach toxins into the water that get into the food chain. Animals like whales or sea birds can get tangled in the garbage so they can't feed, swim or fly properly. Many animals that wash up on shore have nets or plastic items wrapped around their mouths or fins.

Try It!

Garbage islands make it hard for sea animals to find food. Use the garbage island in your tub to see why. Gently crack an egg and pour it on top of the plastic island. Break the yolk so it disperses. Then swirl the water in the tub. Can you find the little white "string" (called the chalaza) that is attached to the egg white?

The chalaza resembles the larvae of several sea creatures. Many animals feed on ocean larvae, but plastic islands make larvae hard to spot. Animals might go hungry because they can't find their food.

Another problem is that animals sometimes eat toxic bits of plastic by mistake. Sea turtles, for example, often mistake cheese-slice wrappers for jellyfish floating on the water. When they spot their favorite food, chomp! Eating the plastic not only robs them of nutrition, it can also make them sick.

From the Deep Sea Data Banks

Making Water?

Scientists, researchers and people who own saltwater fish as pets frequently make artificial seawater when the real stuff isn't handy. In addition to sodium chloride (the salt you used to make your own water on page 10), they also add magnesium chloride, sodium sulfate and boric acid.

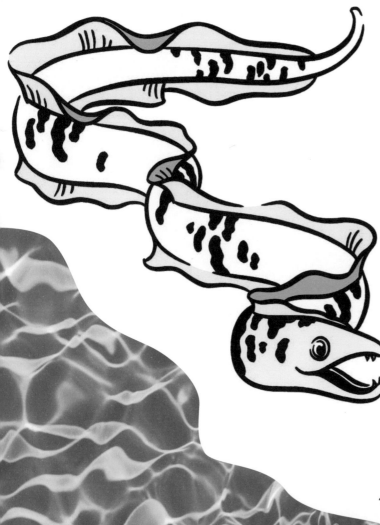

Layer Baked ...

Imagine what would happen if one of the ocean's layers was actually deadly? Wonder no more. Scientists have discovered that in ancient times, the ocean did indeed contain one layer that was so toxic it killed anything that came in contact with it!

According to researchers, around 635–551 million years ago, the oceans were composed of three main layers. The top layer was most like our ocean today — rich in oxygen. The bottom layer was very high in iron. But the middle layer was loaded with dissolved hydrogen sulfide, a deadly gas. Nothing could live in it! This new discovery has changed the way scientists think life may have evolved.

Fish vs. Rubbish

Every year, people dump three times more garbage by weight into the world's oceans than the amount of fish caught.

Current Events

The Gulf Stream is one of the largest convection currents in the Atlantic Ocean. It carries warm water from the tropics up to the western shores of Europe before returning to the equator. That warm water, scientists have long said, has kept nearby countries, like Great Britain, warmer than their less-blessed counterparts at the same latitude, like Russia.

But new research — or should we say the "current" thinking — indicates that this theory may be nothing more than a myth!

Researchers created computer models of ocean currents and land masses at various latitudes. When they tweaked how much heat was carried by the currents in the models, they discovered that the temperature of the nearby land masses did not change. They concluded that the warmer climates of northern regions such as Great Britain or the Northwest Pacific Coast are caused simply by being close to water — any water.

Fun with Magma

Convection currents are at work deep within the Earth, too. To see exactly what happens down in the very basement of Davy Jones' locker, try this twirl-a-world activity.

You Will Need

- scissors
- 2 shoeboxes
- 4 chopsticks
- 2 empty paper towel rolls, cut in half crosswise
- plain white paper
- tape
- ball of thick yarn

1 Cut one short end off each shoe box. With the point of your scissors, poke four holes in each one as shown below.

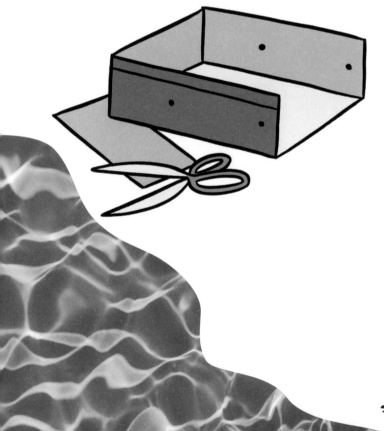

2 Slip one chopstick through a hole. Thread the paper towel tube onto it, then slide the chopstick through the opposite hole. Repeat three more times.

3 Cut the white paper into strips about the same width as your rollers (about 10 cm/ 4 in. wide). You will need a strip that is long enough to go fully around two rollers that are next to each other. If your strip is too short, tape a second strip to it.

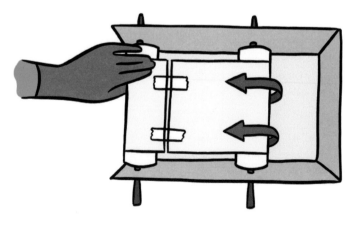

4 Repeat for other pair of rollers.

5 Set the two shoeboxes side by side with the open short sides touching.

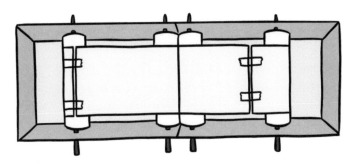

6 Each loop of paper represents a convection current. Turn one of the left-hand rollers counterclockwise. Can you see the convection current moving?

7 Now turn one of the other pair of rollers clockwise, so your two convection currents move in opposite directions.

8 Put the yarn ball beneath the middle two rollers. Pull out the end of the yarn and fold it over a few times. Make a wad thick enough to touch both rollers when you slip it between them.

9 Turn the rollers again. Do the rollers pull the yarn up between them?

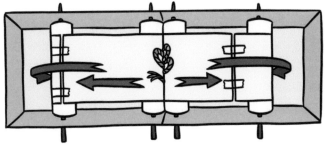

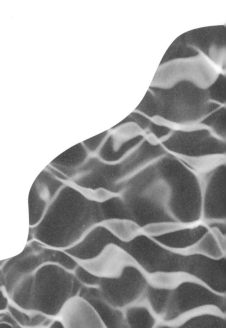

Magma — liquid rock — deep inside the earth circulates by way of convection currents.

What's Going On?

After the invention of sonar, scientists finally had the tools to study the ocean floor. They were amazed to discover a 60 000 km (37 000 mi.) chain of mountains in the middle of the oceans, encircling the entire globe. This mountain range, dubbed the Mid-Oceanic Ridge System, turned out to be the largest geological feature on the planet!

The ridge system holds the key to how Earth's crust moves and changes. The crust is made up of several large "plates." They rest on a semi-liquid ball of molten rock, called magma. The magma is constantly moving, churned by convection currents like the ones in your model.

Deep in the ocean, at the ridge, is where many of Earth's plates meet. The convection currents push the plates apart. Through the vents that open between them, fresh, new rock emerges. The rock hardens and becomes a new piece of the ocean floor. Every year, the ocean floor adds up to 120 mm (4 ½ in.) of new material at its central ridge. As a result, the oceans are gradually getting wider.

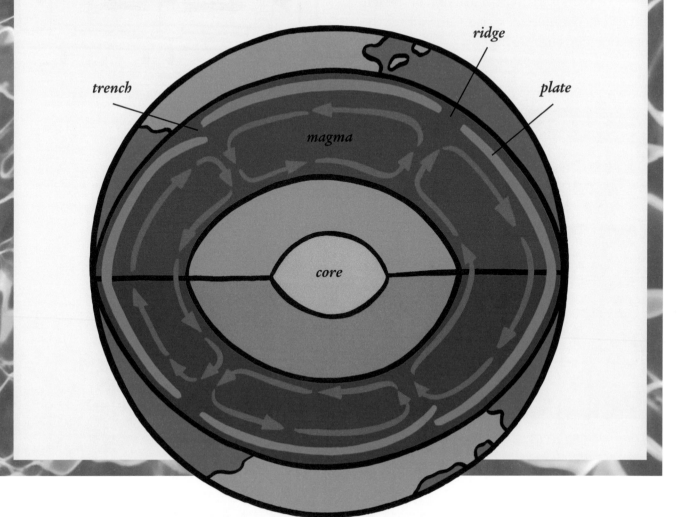

Volcanocean?

Do convection currents in Earth's mantle affect the sea? Make this underwater volcano to see things really heat up.

You Will Need

- a large clear jar (such as a pickle jar)
- ice
- an empty saltshaker
- 10 mL (2 tsp.) salt
- red food coloring
- liquid dish detergent
- 5 mL (1 tsp.) soda pop

1 Fill the jar with cold water and ice.

2 Fill the saltshaker ½ full of hot water. Add the salt, a few drops of food coloring, a few drops of detergent and the soda pop.

3 Screw on its top. Hold your thumb over the saltshaker's holes. Stand the shaker on the bottom of the jar, then let go. Eruption!

What's Going On?

Magma isn't the only thing that erupts from mid-ocean vents. Dissolved gases are released, too (represented by droplets of detergent and soda bubbles). Heat is also released, contributing to the ocean's convection currents and providing energy for marine life.

What's Happening Now?

In 1977, when scientists first observed deep-sea vents, they discovered many previously unknown life forms, including giant tube worms and eyeless shrimp. Together, they formed a complex and complete food chain.

All other known food chains get energy from the sun. But down at the vents, there is no sunlight. So how is this ecosystem powered? It turns out that previously undiscovered bacteria feed on the gases emitted by the vents! The bacteria in turn provide food for all the other animals.

Tsunami!

Make a towering wave in your bathtub — if you dare ...

You Will Need

- scissors
- a plastic lid (such as a large yogurt container lid)
- 60 cm (24 in.) string
- a variety of small objects to serve as houses (such as Monopoly houses, bottle caps, marbles)

1 Poke a hole in the plastic lid. Push the string through the hole and tie a large knot.

2 Run the bathtub tap until there's about 2.5 cm (1 in.) of water at one end of the tub, but the other end is still dry. The wet end is your ocean. The dry end is your beach.

3 Place a few houses on the beach.

4 Place the plastic lid into the water over the closed drain. It should lie flat on the bottom of the ocean.

5 With a smooth, sharp tug on the string, pull the lid straight up. Tsunami!

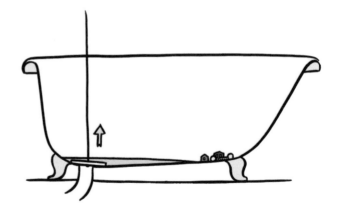

What's Going On?

Earthquakes can move the ocean floor the same way your lid moves — straight up! The motion forms an unusually large wave called a tsunami that hits land with incredible force. Anything in its path gets tossed or smashed — which is exactly what happened when devastating tsunamis hit parts of Asia in 2004 and again in 2011.

The Indian Ocean tsunami in December 2004 was triggered by a 9.2 magnitude quake — the largest ever recorded. The earthquake sent waves up to 30 m (100 ft.) high smashing into shore and up to 2 km (1 mi.) inland. Hundreds of thousands of people died and millions more had their lives shattered. The hardest hit countries were Indonesia, Sri Lanka, India and Thailand.

The March 2011 tsunami was triggered by a 9.0 magnitude quake only 81 km (130 mi.) off the coast of Japan. It sent waves reaching up to 38 m (125 ft.) along a 2100 km (1300 mi.) stretch of Japan's northeastern coastline, reaching up to 10 km (6 mi.) inland.

What's Happening Now?

After the 2004 tsunami, people built an early warning system around the Indian Ocean. Other early warning systems have been set up in the Atlantic, the Mediterranean and the Caribbean as part of a global network to protect coastal dwellers.

Tsunami warning systems work like this:
1. Sensors that measure changes in water pressure are placed on the seafloor. Additional sensors that measure wave height are placed in floating buoys near each seafloor sensor. Together, the sensors can tell when an unusually large wave is passing through that part of the ocean.
2. When sensors show significant changes to water pressure and wave height, they emit signals.
3. The signals are sent to a satellite, which then relays them to an early warning center. From there, staff can quickly

spread information about the tsunami. If tsunami warning systems work properly, people can evacuate threatened areas well before the wave is even visible from land.

Add Is Bad

Water flowing into the ocean isn't always clean. What happens when different pollutants mix?

You Will Need

- a thin sponge
- 20 cm (8 in.) string
- large glass jar (such as a pickle jar)
- 30 mL (2 tbsp.) each: soil, brown sugar, pancake syrup, salt
- 5 mL (1 tsp.) each: pepper, tiny paper scraps, margarine, liquid dish detergent
- food coloring (red, yellow and green)
- mixing spoon

1 Cut the sponge into a fish shape. Tie one end of the string around Flounderella's middle.

2 Fill the jar ¾ full of water. Put Flounderella in. Use the string to help her swim. *How is Flounderella?*

3 Dump the soil into the water. This represents topsoil, which erodes under intensive farming. The soil gets into rivers and washes into the sea.

4 Agricultural runoff usually includes fertilizers. When they reach the ocean, fertilizers speed algae growth. Dead algae sinks to form a sludge. Pour brown sugar into the jar to represent sludge.

5 Oil spill! Pour pancake syrup into the jar to represent oil.

6 In cold regions, people often use salt to melt ice and keep roadways clear. The salt winds up in the ocean, so pour it in!

7 Improperly disposed garbage ends up in the ocean, too. Pour the pepper and paper scraps into the jar.

8 Human and animal wastes also wind up in the ocean. Dump the margarine in.

9 Factories sometimes produce waste, too. Add dish detergent to simulate factory waste. Add two drops of each food coloring to represent toxic chemicals in the waste.

10 Mix your "ocean." *Would you like to swim with Flounderella?*

The Ocean at Risk

During the 1960s and 1970s, the St. Lawrence River became heavily polluted. The local beluga whales showed high rates of cancer. When they died, their bodies were so contaminated that they had to be disposed of as toxic waste!

In 1983, the river's beluga population hit its lowest point. The Canadian government put the whale on its endangered species list. Aggressive efforts to clean the river and save the whales began.

Those efforts paid off. In 2004, the St. Lawrence beluga's status changed from endangered to threatened. While the population is still low, the beluga is no longer in danger of extinction.

What's Going On?

When you lift out Flounderella, you'll see some effects of pollution. Her color may have changed, and she will be covered with gunk. You'll also see changes in the water itself.

There are many changes you *can't* see, though. Flounderella's body is struggling against the toxic effects of the chemicals. She's also gasping for breath — there's less oxygen thanks to the algae sludge on the ocean floor. And she's working harder to find food — there's less sunlight because of the dirt in the water, and Flounderella lives on light-loving phytoplankton.

Chemicals in the water also interact to form new chemicals. These may be more damaging than any of them alone. For example, mercury slows the breakdown of oil and makes it more toxic.

Ka-Boom?

If you think cleaning your room is hard, imagine cleaning up an oil spill. Since oil floats, it's hard to predict where it will spread. Once it hits land, it's even more difficult to clean up.

Want to stop a spill in its tracks? Try mopping up the slick stuff using a homemade oil boom.

You will need:

- glass baking dish
- blue food coloring
- small mixing bowl
- 90 ml (6 tbsp.) vegetable oil
- 60 ml (4 tbsp.) cocoa powder
- assorted absorbent materials: e.g., paper towels, cotton balls, rags, nylon pot scrubber, styrofoam cup, sponges, peat moss (from a garden supplier)
- assorted breakfast cereals: e.g., shredded wheat, puffed rice, puffed wheat, puffed corn

1 Fill the baking dish halfway with water. Add the food dye and stir. This is your "ocean."

2 Using your collection of absorbent materials, construct a floating "boom" — a barrier that absorbs oil and prevents it from spreading. Place the boom in the dish so it blocks off one side.

3 In your small bowl, mix together 45 ml (3 tbsp.) vegetable oil with 30 ml (2 tbsp.) cocoa. The mixture represents crude oil.

4 *Very slowly*, pour the "crude oil" into one side of the baking dish. Your aim is to get the mixture to float on top of the water.

5 How well does your boom keep the other side of the "ocean" clean?

6 Clean out the dish and repeat your experiment using the breakfast cereals to make your boom. Do the cereals absorb more or less oil?

What's Going On?

Many tools are used to clean up spills. One is an absorbent boom like the ones you made. Some booms are even made of — yes — Rice Krispies. The specially treated cereal forms semisolid blobs that can be scooped off the water. They can then be compressed to recover the oil.

The downside is that booms sop up water along with oil. Another tool, called a skimmer, scoops oil *off* the water's surface. Skimmers are the least destructive to the environment, but they can only remove 15 percent of the oil.

A third method uses chemicals to break up the oil. When droplets of oil are small enough, bacteria can eat them and naturally break them down. Special types of bacteria may even be added to the water to speed the process along.

A final method for cleaning up oil is to burn it. While this can remove up to 98 percent of oil from the water, the smoke and heat produced can be damaging in its own right. None of the methods for cleaning up spills work perfectly. That's why it's better to avoid spilling gunk into the sea in the first place.

The puffy orange boom corrals oil on the surface of the water where it can then be skimmed off.

Oil and Water Don't Mix

Every year, more than 2650 million L (700 million U.S. gal.) of oil get into our oceans. About half comes from land (for example, from the improper disposal of waste, such as used motor oil). A lot comes from the normal upkeep of ships (nearly 20 percent). But occasionally, accidents result in huge amounts of oil being spilled into the sea. Major spills like these can have catastrophic effects on the sea and its inhabitants.

During the first 48 hours of an oil spill, 30–40 percent of the oil evaporates. These are the most toxic and flammable parts of the oil, so any living thing exposed to the evaporating oil can be severely harmed.

Most of the oil that's left behind floats, forming a film on the water's surface about 0.1 mm (1/250 in.) thick. It keeps spreading and getting thinner until it is just a sheen — a rainbow-filled film about .001 mm (1/25 000 in.) thick. A tiny percentage of the oil may sink, especially if it has mixed with sand or algae.

In 2010, an explosion damaged the wellhead of an offshore drilling platform in the Gulf of Mexico. Over three months, more than 760 million L (200 million U.S. gal.) of crude oil spilled into the ocean.

The spill affected more than 11 000 square km (4200 square mi.) of ocean habitat and 510 km (320 mi.) of American coastline. Immense underwater plumes of dissolved oil were reported after the disaster. A 210 square km (80 square mi.)

"kill zone" developed on the ocean floor around the well site. All visible life disappeared.

No one knows what the long-term consequences of the spill will be. Chemicals used to break up the oil have their own toxic effects. They have been found in the larvae of certain crabs, meaning they have gotten into the food chain. Cancer-causing substances in the oil may also affect many organisms that feed or breed in the area. Methane, a gas released in the spill, may also create "dead zones" devoid of oxygen in the Gulf. And miles-long strings of weathered oil and tarballs are an ongoing risk to thousands of migrating birds, especially ducks and geese.

As a result of the spill, countries like the United States and Canada are revisiting their policies for oil drilling at sea. While new rules controlling offshore drilling may reduce the risk, getting oil from deep beneath the ocean floor will always be dangerous.

What's Happening Now?

During the Gulf spill, skimmer boats dragged fishnets containing special mops through the oil. The mops were actually MOP (short for Maximum Oil Pickup), a patented material made from 100 percent recycled cellulose fibers. Charles Diamond, who heads the MOP-making company, said,

"One container of MOP sorbent can contain up to 300 000 L (75 000 U.S. gal.) of oil in four hours. It would take about 23 000 booms to get the same results." The MOP can be squeezed or burned to reclaim the oil, and MOP itself is 100 percent biodegradable.

From the Deep Sea Data Banks

Let There Be Life!

Boiling undersea vents are hot, to be sure. But they are also really cool! Some scientists now think that life on Earth may have started in them!

According to Gunter Wachtershauser, the scientist who first proposed the theory, the vents release an important group of chemicals. They can form compounds, like amino acids, that are basic to life.

For life to start, the chemicals need to be contained and concentrated, like they are inside the cells of your body. How could this occur in the free-flowing ocean? Wachtershauser says the unique, porous structure of the rock at the vents acts like artificial cells. Chemicals could have been concentrated and contained in just the right way to allow life to evolve.

If Wachtershauser's theory is right, then the process that shaped life on Earth still goes on today!

Give or Take a Couple of Million ...

Researchers believe that more than half of all life on Earth is found in the ocean. How many species does that figure include? No one knows for sure! To date, 199 146 marine species have been identified. But humans have explored less than 10 percent of the ocean's waters. How many more species exist that no one has ever seen?

The answer might surprise you. Scientists calculate that the total number of species most likely is around 750 000 but may be as high as *25 million!*

Turtle Attraction

Loggerhead sea turtles migrate incredibly long distances across open ocean. Year after year, they return to the exact same beaches to lay their eggs. How on Earth — and in ocean — do they find their way?

Scientists have finally figured out the secret to the turtles' navigation know-how. It turns out they can sense the magnetic field that surrounds Earth. The field varies in strength and angle at different parts of the globe. Able to detect both features, turtles can determine their latitude *and* their longitude — something most researchers did not previously think was possible.

The new findings reveal a lot about turtles and might also help humans learn to navigate the oceans more safely.

Hiding Your Light?

Think there's no light deep in the sea? News *flash!* There *is* — it comes from sea creatures themselves! Discover with a friend how and why glow-in-the-dark animals shine in this "enlightening" experiment.

You Will Need

- white poster paint
- a small paintbrush
- 2 sheets of black poster board
- a pencil
- scissors
- masking tape
- a small mirror

1 Paint tiny white dots randomly on both sheets of poster board. Let dry.

2 Draw a sea animal on one sheet. Give it a "handle" about 20 cm (8 in.) long and 7.5 cm (3 in.) wide. Cut out the fish with its handle.

3 Tape the other sheet of poster board to the wall. Dim the lights. This is your ocean.

4 Ask your friend to make the sea creature "swim" about 15 cm (6 in.) in front of your spotty ocean.

5 Take six giant steps away from the wall. Hold up your mirror so you can see the ocean behind you.

6 Close your eyes and say, "Freeze, fish!" (It's so cold at the bottom of the sea, your fish *is* practically frozen!) Your friend should hold the sea creature as still as possible.

7 Open your eyes. Can you see your sea creature against the dark spotted background, or does it seem to disappear?

What's Going On?

Plants and animals use repeating patterns to camouflage or break up their outlines. That makes them hard to see against busy backgrounds.

In the dark depths of the ocean, animals use *light* to break up their outlines. Most make it themselves, using special light-emitting organs. The organs appear as tiny white dots, just like the dots on your creature.

The lights can be used to confuse predators or prey. For example, loosejaw fish give off red light. The light bounces off prey and back to the loosejaw's eyes, which can detect shades of red. Most other ocean species can't see red, though. To them, the looming loosejaw is invisible. So loosejaws have, in effect, night-vision specs that let them spot their prey and sneak up on them, too.

The Ocean at Risk

The creatures that live in the deepest parts of the ocean are — let's be frank — really weird. But many researchers think that their very weirdness is what supports *all* ocean life!

To survive in the dark, cold depths, animals have to change, or adapt, to cope with the tough conditions. They evolve faster than creatures in less challenging habitats. Eventually, new species arise that are better adapted to conditions *everywhere* in the ocean.

But what happens when conditions in the toughest environments get too tough for even the wildest and wackiest? Scientists say that global warming might make deep waters unlivable. The little oxygen there comes from above, when ocean currents force waters at different levels to mix. Global warming might reduce the amount of vertical mixing, leaving deep waters with too little oxygen to sustain life. The important animals living there would disappear.

Red Fish, Blue Fish, One Fish, Two Fish

Marine creatures are camouflage experts. Make these undersea goggles and play fishy hide-n-*sea*k with a friend.

You Will Need

- a pencil
- poster board
- scissors
- 2 strings 30 cm (12 in.) long
- blue cellophane
- clear tape
- red construction paper

1 Using the picture above as a guide, draw a pair of goggles on your poster board. Cut them out. Remember to cut out the eyeholes!

2 Poke a hole at each side of the goggles. Thread one string through one hole. Tie a knot to fasten in place. Repeat on the other side.

3 Fold the cellophane in half, and then in half again to make four layers. Cut a strip of layered cellophane to fit inside your goggles. Tape it in place. Tie the goggles behind your head to hold them in place. When you put on the goggles, you should be looking through all four layers of cellophane.

4 Draw several fish shapes on the red paper. Cut them out. Ask your friend to scatter the fish around the room.

5 Dim the lights. Put on your goggles, and go fish! How many critters can you find in a minute?

What's Going On?

Water only lets through some wavelengths of light. Blue passes through most easily. Other colors, like red and yellow, are blocked. That's why large bodies of water often look blue.

Because water blocks red light, red objects don't reflect much light under water. They become, in effect, invisible. This is especially true in deep water and at night.

When you wear blue goggles, you see what animals see under water. Goodbye, red!

Bright Idea

Turn your understanding of camouflage upside down with this experiment.

You Will Need

- glue
- white paper
- black construction paper
- a pencil
- plastic wrap
- scissors
- a large, clear container of water

1 Glue the white paper onto the black. Draw sea animal shapes on the paper. Cut them out.

2 Sandwich the animals between two sheets of plastic wrap. Press to seal.

3 Cut out the animals, leaving enough plastic wrap around their edges to stay sealed.

4 Place the container of water on a dark surface. Float your animals, black side up, in it.

5 Look down on your animals from above. Are they easy to see against the dark bottom? Now look up at them from below. How easy are they to see?

6 Turn half the animals over so their black sides are facing down and their white sides are facing up. Now which animals are easier to see from above? Which are easier to see from below?

What's Going On?

In the ocean, light usually comes from one direction: up. Any animal that looks up from the depths will be looking into brightness. Any animal that looks down will be looking into darker waters.

Animals use a technique called countershading to take advantage of this fact. Countershaded animals have lighter-colored bellies than backs. That makes it harder for predators to spot them, whether they are looking up or down.

The Dark Side of Farming

In much of the world, farmers use chemical fertilizers to help their crops grow. When it rains, the fertilizers wash into rivers and streams. Eventually, they wind up polluting the ocean.

Microscopic plants called algae feed on the nutrients — phosphates and nitrates — in the fertilizers. They multiply like mad. The result? An algal "bloom" that can cover vast areas of the ocean's surface.

With so much algae on the water's surface, less light reaches below. But many sea creatures rely on light to help them find prey. Seahorses, for example, have trouble finding food when there is less sunlight. Reduced light also harms sea grass, which needs sunlight to make food. Many prey animals, like the snake pipefish, depend on sea grass for camouflage. So fertilizer runoff harms plants, predators and prey far from the farm.

When algae die, they sink to the bottom of the ocean. Bacteria go to work decomposing them. The bacteria consume oxygen. Large amounts of algae and bacteria can remove so much oxygen from the water (called deoxygenation) that there isn't enough for other animals to breathe. They either leave the area or die. The result: a "dead zone."

Scientists first identified human-caused dead zones in the 1960s. Since then, the number and size of the dead zones has *doubled* every decade. Today, there are more than 400 dead zones around the world, covering more than 246 000 square km (95 000 square mi.).

"Dead zones" don't have enough oxygen in them to enable most marine species to live.

The world's largest dead zone is in the Baltic Sea. In North America, the largest zone is in the Gulf of Mexico. Both dead zones are expanding each year.

Experts say the problem, though still growing, is solvable. By using fertilizers more sparingly, preventing sewage from getting into rivers and replanting vegetation along riverbanks, we can stop dead zones from growing out of control.

What's Happening Now?

Dead zones can, and do, disappear. The Black Sea once had the largest dead zone in the world. It totally disappeared between 1991 and 2001, after the region's economy collapsed. Synthetic fertilizers suddenly became too expensive for farmers to use.

When runoff from farmers' fields no longer fueled the dead zone, fish returned *en masse*. Fishing has again become a major industry in the once-dead zone!

Other regions are now reducing the amount of nitrates and phosphates they release into the ocean. In Canada, phosphate detergents were banned in 2010. In the United States, 16 states also moved to ban phosphates in detergents. These bans will stop unnecessary phosphates from contributing to dead zones in our planet's waters.

What Can You Do?
- If detergents with phosphates are still available in your region, don't buy them!
- If you have houseplants or a garden, avoid using chemical fertilizers. Choose natural options, like compost or manure tea, to keep your plants *and* planet healthy.
- Write a letter to your local government representative asking them to support laws that reduce excess fertilizer use and runoff.

Kooky Cukey

Fish don't get waterlogged in water. Find out why when you do this experiment with — *cucumbers?*

You Will Need

- 2 small bowls
- 5 mL (1 tsp.) salt
- a knife
- a cucumber

1 Fill both bowls with water. Stir the salt into one bowl. (You might want to label this bowl so you remember which it is.)

2 Slice eight thin circles from the cucumber. Put four cucumber slices in each bowl.

3 Wait at least 30 minutes. Then examine your cuke slices. Have some become limp and bendy? Which ones?

4 Now switch the slices so the ones that were in the salt water are in the bowl with the freshwater and vice versa.

5 Wait 30 minutes again. What's happened to your cucumbers?

What's Going On?

Water moves in and out of cells by a process called osmosis. It moves from areas that are packed more tightly with water molecules to areas that are less tightly packed.

Cucumber cells are full of water. The water pushes against the cells' walls, making them stiff. That's what gives a cucumber its juicy crispness.

Saltwater is less dense than freshwater. When you place the cucumber slices in saltwater, the water inside the cucumber's cells migrate to the area where the water is less dense — the dish. The result? Floppy, limp cucumber slices that are dehydrated (containing very little water).

Swap the cucumber slices, and you'll see the opposite reaction. Now the salty cucumber slices have lower water density than the freshwater surrounding them.

The water moves from the bowl back into the cucumber slices, plumping them up again.

Fish cells, like cucumber cells (and your cells, too!) contain water. But ocean fish live in saltwater. Their cells constantly lose water because of osmosis. As such, fish that live in the ocean have to drink a lot of water to avoid dehydration. They don't pee very much either — they get rid of excess salt through their gills.

Fish that live in freshwater have the opposite problem. The water in their cells is saltier than the water around them. They constantly absorb more water from the environment than they need. So freshwater fish pee a lot!

The Ocean at Risk

Fish and other marine animals tend to live at specific depths. They are adapted to the amount of sunlight, the water temperature and the amount of salt in the water, called salinity, at that depth. But what happens when these factors change? The North Atlantic, for example, has recently experienced record high temperatures and salinity levels.

Changes in salinity can be a big problem for fish. Getting rid of excess salt takes energy. So if the amount of salt in the water increases, it can be difficult for fish to survive.

No one knows for sure what caused the record-setting changes in the North Atlantic. Some scientists attribute it to global warming, which they think may be altering ocean currents.

Sink or Swim

What keeps fish from floating or sinking? The answer is "in the bag."

You Will Need

- 3 balloons
- 30 mL (2 tbsp.) vegetable oil
- 3 ziplock plastic bags

1 Fill one balloon with water. Don't stretch the balloon — just fill it up. Tie a knot.

2 Blow a little air into the second balloon. Tie a knot.

3 Fill the third balloon with vegetable oil. Tie a knot.

4 Put the air-filled balloon inside a ziplock bag. Fill the bag about half-full with water and seal it. Repeat with the other two balloons and ziplock bags. These bags are your fish.

5 Fill the sink with water. Put all three bags into the sink. Which fish floats the best? Which fish sinks?

What's Going On?

Every type of fish has a preferred habitat. Some live near the surface. Others live deeper in the sea. Some swim up and down, chasing prey at different levels.

To stay at the depths they prefer, fish need to control how buoyant they are. To do so, many have a balloon-like organ called a swim bladder. When the bladder is filled with oxygen, the fish rises toward the surface, just like the bag with the air-filled balloon.

When a fish wants to sink, it releases some oxygen from its swim bladder. The fish sinks, just like the ziplock bag with the water-filled balloon inside it. For the fish to float, the bladder reabsorbs oxygen from its blood. The swim bladder reinflates.

Not all fish have swim bladders. Sharks, for example, have very large livers filled with oil. Oil is lighter than water. That helps keep the shark from sinking completely. But the liver isn't buoyant enough to work unless the shark is actively swimming. That's one reason why sharks never stop swimming — if they do, they'll sink to the bottom of the sea!

Silly Gilly

Got gas? So do the fish in the ocean. Find out how they breathe underwater.

You Will Need

- 2 cups
- 50 mL (1/4 c.) coffee grounds
- a tissue

1 Fill one cup with water. Add the coffee grounds and stir.

2 Place a tissue over the empty cup. Push it down with your fingertips so it makes a sort of pouch.

3 Use one hand to hold the tissue in place. Carefully pour the coffee mixture into the pouch. The pouch should trap the coffee grinds, letting the rest of the water go through.

What's Going On?

The coffee grounds represent oxygen molecules suspended in water. The tissue represents a fish's gills.

When a fish swims, it sucks in large quantities of water. It then forces the water across the gills on both sides of its head. The gills work like the tissue to strain oxygen from the water. Once the oxygen has been captured, the leftover water goes out through the gills.

water is sucked in through the mouth

fish gills

water flows through the gills and out

Old as the Sea

Study fish scales to learn their age-old *sea*cret.

You Will Need

- a cold-water fish with scales (from a grocery store)
- a handheld magnifying glass
- dark paper

1 Use your fingernail to scrape some scales from the fish. Let them dry.

2 Lay the scales on the paper. Examine them through the magnifier. Can you see rings of color, like the rings inside a tree trunk?

What's Going On?

Fish scales grow throughout a fish's life. The scales of fish from temperate-zone waters have color bands that grow wider and lighter each summer. You can see how old the fish was by counting the number of wide bands on each scale.

The Ocean at Risk

You're on an ocean trawler, fishing. You unreel giant fishing nets that scoop up large numbers of fish. They're unloaded on deck in a squirming, wiggling mass, young and old together, along with many other species accidentally trapped. The young fish never got the chance to breed, so fewer fish hatch to replace the ones that are caught. Eventually, the fishery crashes.

This situation has repeated itself time and time again. In 1992, for example, the huge cod fishery off the coast of Newfoundland all but disappeared. The cod, which once numbered in the billions, dwindled to less than 0.001% of their historic levels. The fish that had provided people with livelihoods for hundreds of years was in danger of becoming extinct.

Rules that prevent overfishing are now in place around the world. For example, many areas enforce quotas, limiting how many fish each person can catch at a time. Regulations also limit the size of fish you can catch. So smaller fish are allowed to mature and reproduce. These rules help protect fish stocks for future generations.

Nevertheless, illegal fishing is still a major problem around the world. According to Fisheries and Oceans Canada, 4–9 billion dollars of fish are illegally caught every year. Hardest hit are developing nations, which don't have strong governments or enough money to protect their own waters.

What Can You Do?

- If you fish, follow the rules! Don't keep fish that are smaller than the legal limits.
- Practice catch and release for all fish that you do not plan to eat.
- Having fish for dinner? Stick to fish that are not threatened or endangered. This chart can help you make the best choices.
- Love that tuna sandwich? Choose canned "light" tuna that comes from skipjack tuna fish. This variety of tuna contains lower levels of the toxic chemical mercury than other types of tuna. And it is more likely to be caught using environmentally friendly methods. Look for the words "troll-caught" or "pole-and-line caught" on the label.

AVOID	BETTER CHOICE
Atlantic Cod	Pacific Cod
Atlantic Salmon	Pacific Salmon
Orange Roughy	Mackerel
Atlantic Halibut	Pacific Halibut
Monkfish	Striped Bass
Grouper	Tilapia
Chilean Sea Bass	Herring

How Many Is Too Many?

Your mission: Catch as many fish as you can to feed your family. But how many is too many? Play this game with a friend to find out.

You Will Need

- a bag of M&Ms or other small candy (about 100 pieces)
- goldfish-shaped crackers or similar (about 75 pieces)
- 15 grapes
- 250 mL (1 c.) uncooked rice
- a large bowl
- masking tape
- a pencil
- 2 napkins
- a timer or watch

1 Mix the candy, crackers, grapes and rice in the bowl.

2 Attach 15 cm (6 in.) of masking tape to one end of the pencil so it hangs down like a fishing line.

3 The bowl is the ocean. The napkin is your ship. Your task is to use your rod to catch as many fish as you can in 30 seconds. Shake them onto your ship as you go.

4 When you are done fishing, use the chart (page 51) to calculate the value of your catch. Add up the value of your fish. Subtract the value for the bycatch from your total. Any fish that wind up on the table, not on your napkin, get returned to the sea.

5 You and a friend take four turns each. Each turn represents one year of fishing.

6 At the end of four years, compare how much money you and your friend made each year. Who made the most money? In which year did you both make the most money combined?

7 You need to make 75 dollars every year to feed your family. Did you make this much money every year?

8 Look inside the bowl. Is there less than three of any type of fish? If so, then that species has become "extinct" — there aren't enough left to reproduce.

What's It Worth?

Fish	Represented by	Value
Sardines	candy	$1.00
Bluefish	crackers	$2.00
Yellowfin Tuna	grapes	$10.00
Bycatch (all other marine species)	rice	-$0.05

What's Going On?

Since 1950, the fishing industry has quadrupled the total number of fish caught. According to the United Nations, 15 out of the 17 world fisheries are overfished or depleted. Ninety percent of the large fish species in the oceans have been fished out — there aren't enough to sustain themselves — in the last 50 years.

In this activity, you can see what happens when fishers try to take as much as they can, without thinking of sustainable limits. But there is also the pressure to feed their families and make a living.

While fishing, you accidentally caught other kinds of fish that you didn't want: bycatch. You paid a price for each grain of rice you caught. But in the open ocean, fishers don't pay for bycatch — the ocean does. Large nets can remove fish and other creatures from their habitats, affecting all the other living things in the food chain.

From the Deep Sea Data Banks

Jammin' Salmon

In 2009, the annual salmon run in British Columbia's Fraser River reached an all-time low. Less than 1.5 million fish returned — about 10 million less than expected. But the summer of 2010 delivered a huge surprise — a whopping *34 million* fish returned to the river. They were packed so tightly together that they turned the waters red. It was the largest salmon run since 1903.

While no one can yet fully explain the decline or dramatic return of the sockeye salmon, the 2010 run is cause for hope. It shows that Earth's ecosystems are resilient and can be healed even when there is widespread damage.

The Ocean's Nasal Spray?

Seabirds spend most of their lives in or above the ocean. When they get thirsty, they sip directly from the sea. But seawater is salty. Too much salt can be as bad for birds as it is for human beings. So how can seabirds consume this briny beverage?

Their secret lies in specialized salt glands. The glands remove extra salt from the birds' blood and force it into their sinuses. When enough salt accumulates in a bird's nose, watch out! Ah-ah-ah-*choo!* Whenever the bird sneezes, out comes a blast of salt spray!

Myth or Truth?

Sailors have often told stories about sea serpents. Legend says these giant monsters have long, snakelike bodies, horselike faces — and they bring destruction to anyone who crosses their path.

Of course, these fanciful creatures are just myths. Or are they? Meet the oarfish. The longest bony fish in the world, the oarfish can grow up to 17 m (56 ft.). They have blue gills and a magnificent red fin along their backs.

Oarfish live in deep waters and are rarely seen. In Japan, the appearance of dead oarfish on the beach is considered an ill omen and a warning of an impending earthquake.

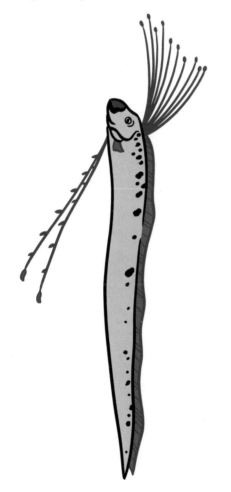

Sniff Test

Otters eat all kinds of prey, many of which are hidden in rocky crevices. So how do they find food that they can't see or feel in the ocean depths? They smell them!

In 2006, wildlife photographer Charlie Hamilton James read a study showing that star-nosed moles have a keen sense of smell — even underwater. They do this by exhaling into the water and then sniffing the air bubbles back in. The air picks up scent molecules, which the moles can detect without breathing in the water itself.

James had a hunch that otters did the same thing. So he used infrared light to film an otter feeding in the dark. The otter swam directly toward a dead trout and gobbled it without hesitation, even though he couldn't see it.

James analyzed the footage. Sure enough, the otter had exhaled a small air bubble. The bubble touched the prey before being sniffed back by the otter!

Spoil Spill

Birds of a feather stick together in this gross, greasy experiment.

You Will Need

- a cup
- 45 mL (3 tbsp.) vegetable oil
- 15 mL (1 tbsp.) cocoa
- 2 large bowls of water
- assorted feathers (from a craft shop)
- a dishcloth
- liquid dish detergent

1 Mix oil and cocoa to simulate crude oil. Very slowly, pour the mixture into one of the water-filled bowls. Your aim is to get the oil to float on top of the water.

2 Start with a clean feather for each bowl, and run them through the tests in the left-hand column of the chart on page 55. Record your observations.

3 Wipe off the oily feather. Get it as clean as you can. Repeat your tests in the clean water. Do your results change?

4 Squeeze a few drops of dish detergent into the oily water. Repeat your tests with the oil-and-detergent. What happens?

What's Going On?

Feathers are totally cool.

Actually, that's not true. They're *warm*. Their shapes, especially those close to the body (called *down*), allow them to trap air. The air is warmed by body heat and acts as an insulator. That's how a down jacket or duvet keeps you warm, too.

Feathers also keep a bird dry. Most birds have a gland near their tails that produces oil. When a bird grooms itself, it spreads the oil over its feathers. The oil repels water, letting it literally roll off its back.

Feathers are made of a material called keratin — stuff that's similar to your fingernails. It's very strong and very light. That's what allows birds to fly. The less a bird weighs, the less energy it needs to stay aloft.

When feathers get covered with oil, like during an oil spill, they can't do their jobs. Their "branches" stick together, so they can't trap much air for insulation. Water no longer rolls off the feathers, either. Instead, it spreads out, weighing down the bird. That makes it harder for birds to stay dry, and to fly.

When you squirted detergent into the oily water, you may have noticed the oil broke up into smaller blobs. Normally, oil and water don't mix. Their molecules repel each other, so they separate into distinct layers. But detergent changes things. One end of the detergent molecule is attracted to water. The other is attracted to oil. When you put all three substances together, the detergent acts like a bridge, allowing water and oil to connect. Once joined, the oil no longer forms a single layer. It can form tiny droplets, suspended in the water. The smaller droplets wash away more easily.

	CLEAN FEATHER		OILY FEATHER	
	WATER	CRUDE OIL	WATER	CRUDE OIL AND DETERGENT
Lay the feather on the water. Does it float or sink?				
Remove the feather. Is there water on it? Does it bead up or spread around?				
Shake the feather. Does the water easily roll off?				
Blow on the feather. Does it lift and flutter or hang limply?				

Blubber Gloves

Birds have feathers to stay warm and dry. But what do whales and other marine mammals use for overcoats? Find out with this *coooooool* experiment.

You Will Need

- a package of vegetable shortening
- 2 large ziplock bags or plastic grocery bags
- ice
- a rubber band

1 Dump the vegetable shortening inside one of the plastic bags. Close the bag and squish it around from the outside with your fingers, so the inner surface of the bag is covered and the shortening is evenly distributed.

2 Fill the sink with cold water. Add ice.

3 Put your hand inside the clean plastic bag. Slip your plastic-covered hand inside the bag of shortening. Fasten both bags tightly around your wrist with the rubber band. (You might need a friend's help.)

4 Stick both hands into the icy water. Keep them in the water until it gets too cold to bear. Can you keep the blubber-gloved hand in longer than the ungloved one?

What's Going On?

Whales and most other marine mammals have a layer of fat, called blubber, under their skin. The blubber is great insulation. It keeps the animal warm even in very cold water, just like the vegetable shortening kept your bagged hand warmer than your ungloved one.

Unlike whales, sea otters don't have blubber. They have incredibly dense fur — 150 000 hairs per square cm (1 million per square inch) to keep them warm. When resting, they lie on their backs with their paws sticking out of the water. Their paws aren't furry, so this keeps them from getting wet and cold.

What's Happening Now?

Whales and other marine mammals are very intelligent. Like people, they are very social and live for a long time. Every year, they migrate long distances to breed and feed in vastly distant regions of the globe.

Nevertheless, many of these animals — especially dolphins and orcas — are kept in captivity. Some are endangered because of whaling and habitat loss. By keeping the animals, scientists can study them to help protect them. The animals also entertain and educate the public, who might otherwise never get to see these magnificent creatures.

But at the same time, most marine mammals, especially orcas, don't do well in captivity. They don't live as long as orcas in the wild. Many people think it's wrong to keep such intelligent, active creatures in water tanks where they cannot move freely through the oceans.

Whether or not marine mammals should be confined is an ongoing debate. *What do you think is the right thing to do?*

Whale Music

Want to hear what it might be like to hunt at sea? Grab some friends to play this whale of a game.

You Will Need

- an open space in which you can move around freely and safely
- a blindfold

1 Before you begin, make sure everyone knows the boundaries of the game area and that there are no obstacles to trip over.

2 Choose one friend to be the whale. Blindfold him or her. Everyone else is prey and should spread out around the whale.

3 To begin, the whale will make a funny noise — like a beep or growl. The prey animals must echo the sound made by the whale.

4 The whale can take as many steps as he or she likes in any one direction. The prey animals can't move.

5 When the whale has finished moving, he or she makes the funny sound again. All the prey animals must echo the sound.

6 Play continues until the whale catches all its prey. The last animal caught becomes the whale in the next round.

7 To make the game more challenging, both the whale and the prey animals can keep moving, as long as everyone walks — no running!

What's Going On?

Whales are social animals. They swim with groups, or pods, of other whales. They communicate with each other by making deep sounds that travel well through water. They also use sounds to locate prey — a technique called echolocation. Like bats, the whales repeat sounds as they hunt. The sounds bounce off prey. The whale can hear and feel the echoes. They tell the whale not only what kind of animal it is, but also where it is. The whale can then zero in for the attack.

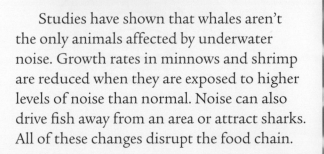

The Ocean at Risk

Thousands of ships with noisy motors travel through the world's oceans every day. Oil exploration, naval operations and other kinds of human activity add to the noise level. In fact, the noise level in the ocean increased by ten times between 1950 and 1975, and is still growing.

How does all this noise affect animals like whales that depend on sound to communicate and find food? Many animals need to expend more energy to survive. Whale songs, for example, get louder and last longer when noisemaking instruments, like a submarine's sonar devices, are on. In essence, whales are forced to shout to be heard over the underwater hubbub. Some whales can also be deafened by excessive noise.

Studies have shown that whales aren't the only animals affected by underwater noise. Growth rates in minnows and shrimp are reduced when they are exposed to higher levels of noise than normal. Noise can also drive fish away from an area or attract sharks. All of these changes disrupt the food chain.

Dinner Time!

**Get out the knife, fork and ... toothbrush?
Yup. It's dinnertime in the Marine Café.**

You Will Need

- a bowl of water
- diced carrots, cheese cubes or other small edibles
- ground pepper
- a fork
- a toothbrush

1 Drop the carrots in the water. These are seals. Sprinkle pepper on the water. The pepper is krill.

2 Use the fork to try and collect either seals or krill from the water.

3 Try again, this time using the toothbrush. Which tool works better for each kind of food?

What's Going On?

There are two types of whales. Toothed whales, like orcas, feed on large animals like seals, fish or penguins. Their teeth resemble the tines of a fork, which can spear their prey.

Baleen whales, like humpback whales, feed on tiny animals called krill. Instead of using teeth to spear them, they use their baleen — a bristly, sieve-like structure — to strain krill from the water.

The Ocean at Risk

Krill are the base of the food chain, a keystone species. But changing conditions in the ocean put krill at risk. Pollution caused by burning fossil fuels is making the ocean more acidic. Researchers have found that the more carbon dioxide in water (a measure of acidity), the fewer krill larvae survive to adulthood. Efforts to find out exactly how much carbon dioxide the krill can tolerate — and methods to protect them — are ongoing.

Pricky Eater?

Can you make like an otter and eat a sea urchin without getting pricked?

You Will Need

- 15 mL (1 tbsp.) cream cheese
- a plate
- pretzel sticks

1 Mold the cheese into a ball. Flatten it slightly against the plate.

2 Stick the pretzels into the cheese on all sides so it resembles a sea urchin

3 Now try to eat the non-spiny, soft bits at the bottom of the urchin without getting stuck. Use your imagination to figure out how!

What's Going On?

Otters have a varied diet. They eat oysters, clams, sea urchins and fish. Some otters can be picky eaters. They'll eat only their favorite foods, even when other food is easier to find.

One of the sea otters' fave foods is the sea urchin. But sea urchins have long sharp spines that can release pain-causing toxins, so otters need to avoid the spines while eating! Perhaps you figured out how they do it: Did you use a tool to turn your urchin over?

Otters are the only mammals, other than primates, that use tools. They use rocks to dislodge abalones from crevices, to dig clams from the ocean floor, and to turn over or smash open tough or spiny-shelled animals like sea urchins so they can eat the soft-bodied animals inside them.

Shapes and Sizes — More Surprises

Is fat better than flat? Test marine mammal body shapes in this speedy activity.

You Will Need

- string
- scissors
- modeling clay

1 Cut four pieces of string, each about 30 cm (12 in.) long. Tie a knot at the end of each one.

2 Divide the clay into four even lumps. Each should comfortably fit in the palm of your hand. These will be your marine animals.

3 Wrap each lump around the knot of a string. Mold the lumps into the shapes below.

4 Fill a sink with water. Drop your clay blobs into the sink. Line them up at one end, like at the starting line of a race. Choose any two animals to begin. Grab one string in each hand.

5 On your marks, get set, go! Pull both animals to the other side of the sink. Which one is easier to pull through the water?

6 Remove your slower animal from the sink. Choose a second animal to race against your winner in a second heat. Repeat until you only have one animal remaining. Which animal shape is the best swimmer?

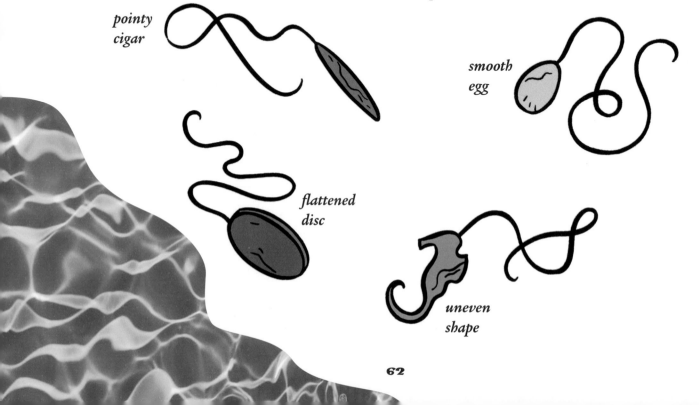

pointy cigar

smooth egg

flattened disc

uneven shape

What's Going On?

It's not easy to swim. As an animal moves forward, it needs to exert lots of energy to overcome friction — the force of the water around it pushing back. Some animals, like fish, have a slimy coating on the outside of their bodies, which helps cut down friction.

Streamlined shapes also reduce friction. A pointier front end cuts through water like a knife through butter. A smooth body, without a lot of bumps and ripples, glides underwater.

Animals that swim long distances tend to be streamlined. Think of a shark or a tuna. Your cigar-shaped lump was most like these animals.

Almost as effective are oval-shaped creatures, like seals, whales and penguins. These animals need lots of fat to keep warm, so they can't be as long and lean as a shark. But they have smooth skins, tapered heads and wings or fins that can press close against their bodies.

Flattened animals, like flounders, can't swim fast, but they are very agile. They can turn quickly to hide under rocks or dart away from predators.

Irregularly shaped animals, like seahorses or lionfish, would also be poor swimmers. Parts that protrude from their body increase friction and slow them down. More rounded animals, like puffer fish, aren't great swimmers either. But many can produce powerful toxins or have sharp spines to keep away predators!

63

How Pearls Are Made

Find out about mollusks in this jewel of an experiment.

You Will Need

- tiny, balled-up piece of paper
- waxed paper
- nail polish (preferably pearlescent white)

1 Lay the paper ball on waxed paper.

2 Cover it on all sides with a thin layer of nail polish. Let dry.

3 Over a period of several days, repeat step 2 several times. Turn the pearl after each application so every side gets evenly covered.

4 Be patient — it can take several weeks to build up a good-sized pearl. A pearl about 0.5 cm (1/4 in.) across can take 30 coats to create.

What's Going On?

Pearls are made by oysters. Oysters are filter feeders. That means they take seawater into their bodies and remove its nutrients before getting rid of the rest.

Sometimes, a parasite enters the oyster along with the water. The invader can harm the oyster's delicate tissues and even kill it. To protect itself from the parasite, the oyster produces a liquid called nacre. Like nail polish, nacre dries to form a hard, shiny coating. Layer upon layer of the protective nacre surrounds the parasite, isolating it so it can't cause any damage. Eventually, a smooth ball is formed: a pearl.

The Ocean at Risk

At one time, the waters along the eastern shores of the United States were so rich with oysters, they were considered junk food. New York City's streets were paved with crushed oyster shells!

But by the middle of the twentieth century, many of the oyster beds were completely fished out. Chesapeake Bay, for example, lost more than 99 percent of its oysters. What oysters remained were too polluted to eat.

The loss of the oyster beds was a tragedy not only for oysters and oyster lovers, but for the ocean itself. Filter feeders, like oysters, help keep the ocean clean. They also build large reefs, like coral reefs, that form protective habitats for many other species.

In recent years, anti-pollution regulations and changes in fishing practices have helped oysters make a comeback. One type of oyster, thought to have become extinct in 1957, has now returned to Scotland's Firth of Forth.

What's Happening Now?

As scientists and researchers wrestle with the problem of protecting oceans from polluted runoff, the humble oyster may provide the answer. In New York City, a project to reestablish oyster beds in Jamaica Bay will also help clean up the city's waterways. Since oysters consume algae, they help reduce oxygen depletion in the water. Scientists are hoping that by reintroducing oysters to the bay, they will clean the water well enough to attract fish and other aquatic life back to the city.

At oyster farms like this one, scientists "seed" oyster larvae into beds made of dangling ropes. They are harvested when they reach maturity.

A Moving Experience

Get a leg up on understanding how sea stars and other echinoderms get around.

You Will Need

- a turkey baster
- a balloon

1 Fill the baster with water.

2 Slide the balloon over the tip of the baster.

3 Hold the baster upright so the balloon-covered tip is touching your work surface.

4 Holding the balloon firmly in place, squeeze the bulb of the baster. The balloon will fill with water. What direction does the turkey baster move?

What's Going On?

Sea stars and other echinoderms have hundreds of water-filled structures called tube feet on the undersides of their bodies. Each tube foot is a lot like your balloon-tipped baster. There's a fat bulb-shaped muscle, called an ampule, at the top end. When the bulb contracts, water is forced down the tube. The tissues at the end of the tube expand and become rigid. The tube foot gets longer. When the ampule relaxes, the water is pulled back. The end of the foot shrinks and looks more like a suction cup.

Tube feet help an echinoderm walk in two ways. When expanded, they act like levers to push the animal along. When retracted, the suction cup at the end of each foot gives the animal better grip so it can control its motions. Also for grip, the tube foot secretes a kind of glue when it expands. Another chemical breaks the attachment when the foot retracts.

Tube Foot Game

Grab some friends to see how tube feet work together to move an echinoderm along the ocean floor.

You Will Need

• a ball

1 Lie down side by side. You are all tube feet.

2 Bend your knees so the soles of your feet are on the floor. When you are in this position, you are retracted tube feet. Your actual feet are the suction cups on the ends of the tube feet.

3 Put the ball at the feet of the last player in line. He should extend his legs and grab the ball between his feet. He must pass the ball to the next player in line. Once done, he can put his feet back on the ground.

4 The second player should extend her legs to grab the ball and move it along to the next player.

5 Continue until the ball reaches the end of the line. How quickly you can pass the ball from one end to the other when you work together?

What's Going On?

Tube feet have to work together. A tube foot extends and sticks to whatever lies beneath. It then angles itself to shift its position. The next tube foot in line then extends and repeats the action. When tube feet move in a synchronized, orderly pattern — like fans doing the wave in a stadium — the animal can slowly drag itself from place to place.

Stuck on Cephalopods

Can _you_ escape from an octopus's suction cups?

You Will Need

- 3 small suction cups with hook attachments
- a rubber band

1 Hold the suction cups with the hooks together.

2 Wrap the rubber band around the hooks to fasten the suction cups to each other.

3 Press the suction cups against a smooth surface. How hard do you have to pull to remove the suction cups?

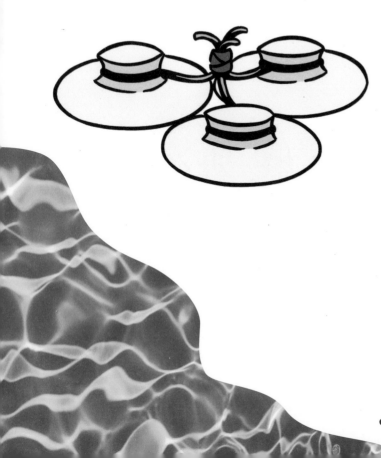

What's Going On?

Air pressure is what makes suction cups hold things fast. Normally, air on both sides of an object presses in on it equally. But when you push suction cups against a flat surface, you squish the air out from beneath the curved cups. The soft, elastic material of the cup make a tight seal, so no air can get in or out.

Air on the outside of the cups presses in, holding them down. There's no air inside the sealed cup to push back, so the cup stays stuck until you exert force — a sharp tug — or break the seal.

An octopus's muscular arms are lined with suckers. They work a lot like the suction cups you used, but they're more sophisticated. Muscles can tighten or relax to adjust the seal on uneven surfaces. They also can change the shape of the space inside the cup to increase the pressure after they have gripped an object. That makes it even harder for prey to get away once they've been grabbed.

Squid have suckers much like an octopus, with one difference — the squid's suckers have little toothy edges that bite into whatever they grab!

What's Happening Now?

Does each octopus arm have a mind of its own? Many researchers think so. While octopuses have very large brains, it turns out about half of their nerve cells — the cells that brains are made of — are actually found in their arms!

Researchers have observed that when an octopus is placed in a tank with food, some of the arms investigate the food by reaching toward it. Other arms, however, behave in exactly the opposite way — they cower in the corner and stay as far from the unfamiliar food as possible. This might happen because the octopus literally can't make up its "minds." The nerve cells in each arm "think" for themselves, like mini brains. Each arm, therefore, can behave differently from the others.

Jet Squid

Squid are among the fastest invertebrates on Earth. They can zoom through the water at speeds up to 40 km/h (25 m.p.h.). Discover how with a friend!

You Will Need

- a balloon
- an empty water bottle with nozzle

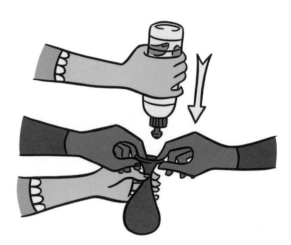

1 Fill the balloon with water. Hold the neck tightly closed.

2 Have your friend stretch the neck of the balloon over the bottle top. Make sure the nozzle is closed when you do this.

3 Fill your sink. Hold your model squid underwater at one end of the sink. Point the head — the balloon — in the direction you want your squid to travel.

4 Pull open the nozzle on the cap. Watch your squid go!

What's Going On?

When a squid wants to move, it sucks water into its body. Then it releases the water through its funnel, a ring of tissue that a squid can aim in any direction, like a fire hose. The water shoots out; the squid jets in the opposite direction. Finlets around the squid's body help control its movement.

Some squid even use their funnels as water pistols. They shoot a powerful stream of water at a predator or prey to stun them! Other species use their fins and funnels to fly. They blast themselves out of the water and flap their fins. They can travel up to 60 m (200 ft.) through the air!

Hide and Ink

Squid are hard to find, unless you're a *sea*-rious scientist.

You Will Need

- a pen or pencil
- paper
- a glass bowl
- green food coloring

1 Trace this squid outline on your paper.

2 Lay the picture on your work surface, and place the glass bowl on top of it. Fill the bowl with water.

3 Squirt a few drops of food coloring into the water to make a blob the same size and shape as the squid. It's not easy, is it?

What's Going On?

When a squid wants to camouflage or escape from a predator, it releases ink into the water. The ink is made of melanin (the stuff that gives your skin its color) and mucous (the stuff that makes snot so snotty). The ink acts like a smoke screen, hiding the squid behind its dark cloud.

But that's not all! Squid also shoot ink in a specific shape — one that resembles their own bodies! That's called a pseudomorph, a word from the Greek meaning "fake body." The ink blob looks so squidlike in dark water that predators sometimes go for it — and get a mouthful of black snot for their trouble!

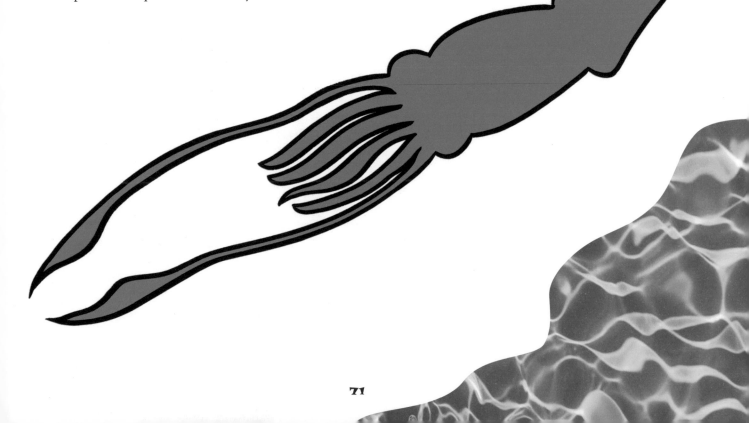

Spots?

Make your own octopus skin in less time than it takes for an octopus to blush.

You Will Need

- a large sheet of newspaper
- 2 sheets of waxed paper about 30 cm (12 in.) square
- food coloring

1 Lay the newspaper on your work surface to protect it.

2 Lay down one sheet of waxed paper. Can you see the grayish newspaper through it? That's the color of your octopus skin.

3 Staying away from the edges of the waxed paper, carefully place 10–20 drops of food coloring on the waxed paper about 1 cm (1/2 in.) apart. Can you still see the gray newspaper between the colored dots?

4 Hold the second sheet of waxed paper above the first sheet. Gently place it on top of the first sheet. See how the spots seem to spread out? Gently press on them with your thumb to spread them out even more. Can you still see the gray newspaper? Or does your octopus skin look yellow?

5 Lift the top sheet of waxed paper off the bottom sheet. Do the dots return to their original size?

What's Going On?

An octopus can camouflage to hide from prey or predators by changing its colors. Many scientists think octopus also use color to communicate and express emotions, such as fear or dominance.

But how do our wriggly friends achieve this tint-o-riffic trick? Octopus skin contains microscopic pigment-filled structures called chromatophores, represented here by the dots of food coloring. Real chromatophores are so small, you can't usually see them.

When an octopus wants to change its hue, it changes the size and shape of its chromatophores. Your thumb, forcing the dots to expand, acts like the small muscles in the octopus's skin. They pull on the chromatophores to widen them. Now the skin they're in is filled with color!

When the octopus relaxes, the chromatophores shrink back to their normal size. The octopus's skin returns to its original color.

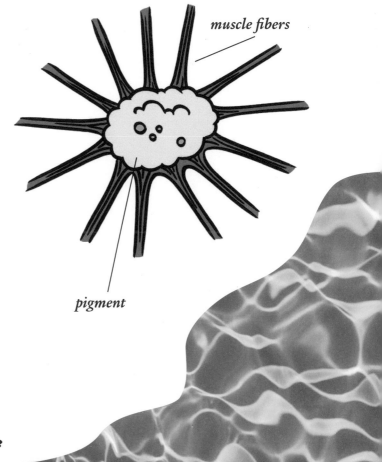

muscle fibers

pigment

Zip! Zap! Zing!

What puts the zing in a jellyfish sting? Find out when you make this zippy model.

You Will Need

- scissors
- a rubber band
- a toothpick
- a turkey baster

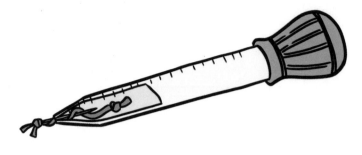

1 Cut the rubber band to make a single, long strand. Tie a knot around one end of the toothpick with it.

2 Tie a knot in the other end of the rubber band. This knot should be small enough to fit into the tip of the baster, but large enough to graze its sides. Wrap the rubber band around the toothpick.

3 Fill the bulb of the baster partway with water. Then stick the un-knotted end of the toothpick, along with the knotted end of the rubber band, into the baster.

4 Hold the turkey baster parallel to the ground, and squeeze the bulb. *Zaaaap!* Your stinger should shoot out the end of the baster, but remain attached by the knot inside the baster.

What's Going On?

Jellyfish have long, fluttery tentacles lined with thousands of "stingers" called nematocysts. The nematocysts are like tiny, spring-loaded harpoons. When they fire, they release a powerful toxin that paralyzes their prey.

Each nematocyst is a fluid-filled capsule, a lot like the bulb of your baster. The neck of the capsule — called a butt! — is pushed inward, and a barbed thread (represented by the toothpick) is wrapped around it.

When a spine on the outside of the nematocyst brushes up against something, it triggers the capsule to contract. The butt is forced out of the capsule, and the barbed thread shoots out, wrapping around whatever it touches.

Nematocysts pack a lot of punch. When the trigger is released, it takes less than three milliseconds for the butt to be fully ejected. It moves with a g-force of 40 000 — about as fast as a bullet!

This incredible force allows the nematocyst barbs to bury themselves almost a full millimeter into the prey's skin, where its toxin can quickly go to work. With its prey unable to move, the jellyfish can reel in its catch.

What's Happening Now?

Hardly anything can live in the ocean's oxygen-poor dead zones — except jellyfish.

Most scientists believed that the invasion of jellyfish in oxygen-poor waters was a death knell for the habitat. Very few animals eat jellyfish or can survive among them. Scientists thought that once jellyfish arrived in large numbers, there'd be no hope of reestablishing other plant and animal life. But new research indicates that may not be the case. In oceans off the coast of Southwest Africa, a fish called the bearded goby may have adapted to live with dead-zone jellies. During the day, the fish hide in the mud. At night, they come out and feed on jellyfish.

As the number of gobies increase, they attract predators like mackerel or hake. Those fish, in turn, feed larger predators such as birds and sea mammals.

Humpty Dumpty Coral

Excess carbon dioxide from burning fossil fuels is gradually making the oceans more acidic. How might more acidic waters affect coral reefs? See for yourself.

You Will Need

- an egg
- 500 mL (2 c.) white vinegar
- large glass container (to hold the vinegar)
- plastic wrap

1 Break the egg neatly in half. Reserve the egg white and yolk for another purpose (like breakfast!).

2 Measure the vinegar into your container. Place the two halves of the eggshell in the vinegar. Cover the container with plastic wrap.

3 Watch what happens when you place the shells in the vinegar. Do you see bubbles forming around the shells?

4 Leave the container in an area where it won't be disturbed. Then check on your eggshells three days later. Where did they go?

What's Going On?

Eggshells are made out of calcium carbonate, the same mineral that coral polyps use to make their shells. Vinegar — an acid — reacts with the calcium carbonate, removing the carbon from the shell. The carbon combines with oxygen to make the gas carbon dioxide. Those are the bubbles you saw rising from the egg.

With no carbon left in the shell, the shell literally dissolves and disappears. What you see floating in the vinegar is just the soft membrane that lines the eggshell. It is similar to the soft bodies of the corals. Like the egg membranes, the coral bodies would float off without their shells. They'd be totally vulnerable to predators.

What's Happening Now?

Despite their tiny size, corals build structures that are so gigantic they can even be seen from space! To do so, they need just the right conditions. They need water that is the right temperature, clarity and acidity. They need to remain undisturbed. And they need the right kind of base to lay the foundation for the reef.

Today, reefs are at risk all over the world. Global warming, ocean acidification, pollution and habitat destruction are all taking their toll. So people are lending corals a helping hand. The Reef Ball Foundation, for example, is a nonprofit organization dedicated to building artificial reefs.

The foundation makes ball-shaped, concrete structures. They lower them in waters where an existing reef has been damaged. Teams of scientists hand "plant" about 500 corals per day onto each structure. The scientists then monitor the growth and health of the corals until the reefs reestablish themselves. The process can take three to five years. Since their founding in 1993, the Reef Ball Foundation has helped rebuild coral reefs in more than 70 countries.

Healthy coral are brightly colored, thanks to algae that live within their cells. Dead or sick coral don't have algae inside them, so they look "bleached," like brittle bones.

The Ocean of the Future

Millions of species of plants and animals call the ocean home: glow-in-the-dark fish, bullet-fast tuna, blushing octopuses. The result is a literal sea of wonders, where corals build mansions, whales sing love songs and oysters make their own glittering jewelry.

Marine species have adapted over millions of years to their watery environment. But today, that environment is endangered. Human-made threats such as global warming, acidification and deoxygenation are changing the composition of the ocean. Those changes can harm all the living things in it — and those on land, too.

Hundreds of thousands of people have already begun taking steps to protect the ocean and its inhabitants. Some are building artificial reefs to help reestablish corals. Others have pushed to reduce the chemical runoff that can cause dead zones. And if you've already tried some of the ocean-friendly tips in this book, such as conserving electricity or water, the number of ocean helpers includes you!

The key to saving the ocean is knowledge. Just 50 years ago, no one had a clue that fiery vents existed at the very bottom of the sea. Today, we know not only about the vents, but also that an utterly unique ecosystem thrives around them. And that's not all — we are learning more and more about the sea every single day.

The more we understand about the ocean and how it works, the better we will be at making decisions about it. We can do things like reseed oyster beds to help clean polluted waters or prohibit fishing methods that damage sea habitats. We can develop new ways to clean up plastic waste or add oxygen to depleted waters.

Much of what we learn in the future will come from you and people like you who care about our planet! So keep learning as much as you can, wherever you can. The ocean's well-being is in your hands, and in the hands of ordinary people everywhere who want to make a difference.

Index